Dirk **Van den Abeele**

the **Lovebird**

A guide to selection, housing,

care, nutrition, behaviour,

health, and mutations

Contents

Foreword

Nothing could be easier than keeping and breeding
birds: you put them in some sort of enclosure, they
take care of their own reproduction and you give
them something to eat and drink now and then.
At least that's the way most people think, until they
try it for themselves and realise that there is more
to it than meets the eye. Keeping and breeding birds
in a responsible manner is an art in itself and fanciers
sometimes take years to discover their ideal system
and accumulate enough know-how to do it
successfully.

Don't forget that birds are living creatures and they
need daily care and attention. Even if you're only
considering keeping one bird, if you don't think you
will be able to devote the time and attention to the
hobby that it demands, it's better for all concerned that
you don't take your plans any further. If there is one
thing the hobby can well do without, it is 'fanciers'
who neglect their animals and give real bird lovers
a bad name. So, to quote an old proverb, "look
before you leap!" This small book will give beginners,
especially, an insight into buying and keeping lovebirds, also known as dwarf parrots.
Breeding is covered briefly, but this varied and
exciting aspect of bird keeping will be handled
in greater detail in a separate publication.

Dirk van den Abeele

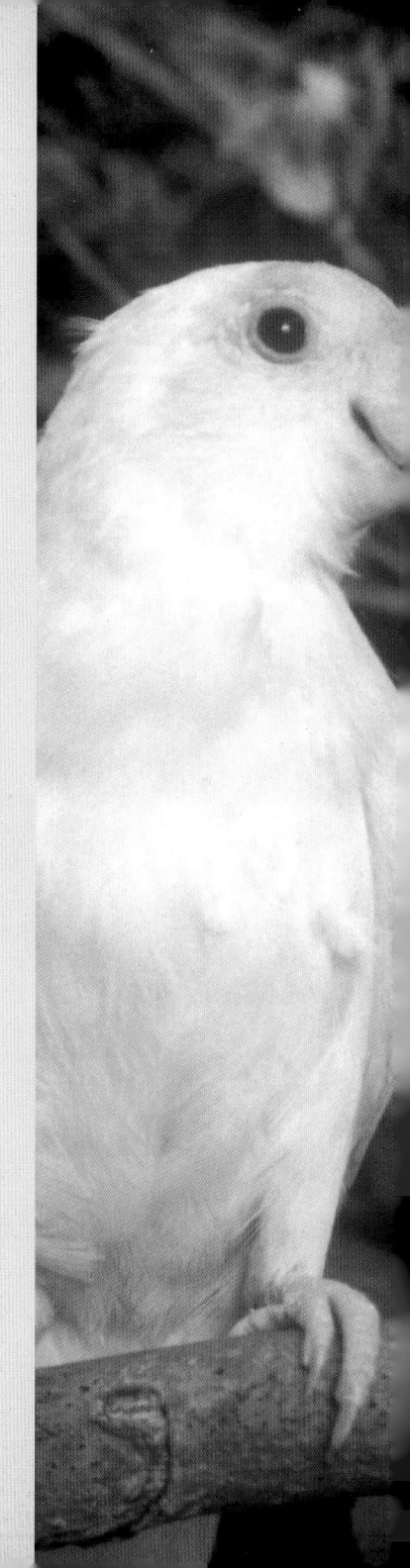

A Publication of About Pets.

ISBN 1852792051
First printing
September 2003

Original title: *de Agapornide*
© 2001 - 2003 Welzo Media Productions bv,
About Pets bv,
Warffum, the Netherlands
www.aboutpets.info

Photos:
Dirk van den Abeele,
Kingdom Books, Rob Dekker
Koos Hammer, BVA

Printed in Italy

General

It's their colours that make them stand out. When these 5 – 6 inch (13 to 16 cm) long birds are busily going about their business they are a feast for the eyes: Agapornis.

Agapornis roseicollis

Almost everyone is acquainted with these amicable African dwarf parrots. In English they are called Lovebirds, in French les inséparables (the inseparable). The name Agapornis originates from the scientific Latin name Agapornis but this was not always their name. In the past Agapornis belonged to the Psittacidae family. It was only in 1836 that Selby reclassified them as a separate genus under the name Agapornis. The name Agapornis is composed from the Greek words agapein (love) en ornis (bird).

Gibberish?

Latin names are used in science and by many animal lovers to tell one type of animal from another with the big advantage that everybody can always be certain of the animal that's involved. A second but equally important advantage is that because the same Latin names are used worldwide mistakes are avoided when buying, selling or exchanging animals or when information is exchanged about them.

The Latin name consists of two or three elements. The first part of the name is the family name or group of animals closely related to one another. All Agapornis belong to the *genus Agapornis*. The second element of the name in combination with the first indicates the species. *Agapornis taranta* is therefore a species. If sub-species exist this is indicated by a third element. *Agapornis taranta nana* is therefore the sub-species of *Agapornis taranta*.

Frequently recurring generic names are often abbreviated in print to save space: *Agapornis taranta* then becomes *A. taranta*. Latin names are often printed in italics.

New names

The importance of using the correct Latin name has already been mentioned but, over the passage of time, names occasionally change and create confusion (see previous page). The majority of changes took place in the 19th and in the first half of the 20th centuries but scientists still sometimes change a name today. During a conference a few years ago, eminent ornithologists concluded that the names *cana*, *pullaria*, *personata* and *swinderniana* were incorrect and decided to use the names *Agapornis canus*, *A. pullarius*, *A. personatus* and

A. swindernianus. Although the majority of fanciers still talk about the cana and the personata we have chosen to use the official names.

Cana:	*A. canus*
Personata:	*A. personatus*
Pullaria:	*A. pullarius*
Swinderniana:	*A. swindernianus*

Family relations

In total there are nine different species of Agapornis:
A. pullarius, A. canus, A. taranta, A. swindernianus, A. roseicollis, A. personatus, A. fischeri, A. nigrigenis and *A. lilianae.*
A number of these species also have sub-species that result in us being able to recognise fifteen different species and sub species of Agapornis. The nine species, also known as 'nominate species' are divided into three groups.

A. canus

A. personatus, blue

A. pullarius

The first group is the so-called sexually dimorphic group. Put simply, this is the group in which the differences between cocks and hens can be seen from their plumage.

Sexually dimorphic group
A. pullarius
A. canus
A. taranta

The second group is a transitional form, between the sexually dimorphic group and the third group.

A. taranta (male)

A. roseicollis,
pale headed lutino

A. fischeri

A. nigrigenis, green

Transitional group
A. roseicollis
A. swindernianus

There is no visible difference between cocks and hens in these two species. Little is known about *A. swindernianus*. In their natural habitat they spend the majority of their time high in the treetops and as a result are rarely found in aviculture. They have never been imported. The *A. roseicollis* is currently the most popular Agapornis and the bird in which the largest number of mutations have appeared.

To conclude, we recognise a third group, namely the group with white-eye rings, also known as 'personata'.

Personata group
A. personatus
A. fischeri
A. nigrigenis
A. lilianae

All members of this group have the typical white-eye rings in common. In this group also there is no visible difference between the cocks and the hens. Because crossbreeding within the group produces fertile hybrids it's possible that the four species evolved from a common parent. This has the advantage that mutations can be passed on from one species to the other, but, and it's a big but, ill-considered crosses only produce hybrids which have no value and endanger the purity of the species.

Lovebird characteristics
• Length: 5 – 6 inches
  (13 – 16.5 cm)
• Average life expectation:
  12 years
• Age sexually mature: average 9 months (because of the risk of egg binding it's preferable to wait until 12 months)
• Egg laying: 3 to 7 eggs (cases of aggression are common so don't leave hatchlings for too long with their parents, if you separate them just before they start to fly they will become tame very quickly)
• Primary colour: green
• Markings: black, yellow, red and blue
• Origin: Africa
• Number of species: 9
• Never imported into Europe:
  A. swindernianus
• Most common species:
  A. roseicollis, *A. personatus*, *A. fischeri*
• Less common species:
  A. lilianae, *A. nigrigenis*, *A. taranta*, *A. canus*, *A. pullarius*

Lovebirds as pets
The facts that most species of lovebird are fairly easy to breed, that there are quite a few colour variations, that some species are relatively inexpensive to buy and that they are relatively undemanding when it comes to food and accommodation has made them the most popular birds of the parrot family. Apart from their popularity as breeding and exhibition birds, lovebirds are also popular pets and they can often be successfully tamed. A large number of breeders have specialised in lovebirds because of their popularity as exhibition birds and a variety of mutations have appeared within the species as a result. The fact that new varieties regularly appear goes to prove that the end of development is still a long way off.

A. personatus, violet

A. fischeri, pastel mauve

A. lillinae

Buying

New owners often follow a common path towards obtaining their first birds: after visiting either an exhibition or a breeder they have become acquainted with, the person decides to keep birds. Somewhere or other this person has an empty shed or space for an aviary.

After a couple of days of activity when the shed or aviary is ready for occupation the person takes a trip to a dealer and in no time at all becomes the proud owner of some pairs. The problems mostly start here: the birds are too old or not racially pure, the accommodation turns out to be too small, eggs are laid but the hatchlings die, and so on. Things would have possibly worked out better if some thought and preparation had been applied in advance.

Before you start
As a beginner it all depends on what you want, a tame parrot as a living room pet that won't simply scream the house down? In this case it's best to choose a young bird that's been hand reared because it will get used to you

quicker. Lovebirds are colony birds and they don't like living completely alone. Birds that are deprived of the company of their own sort can over time develop psychogenic disorders. These are physical sickness symptoms caused by psychological problems and you can best avoid them by buying at least one cock and hen pair.

Not all breeders sell their better birds, so when you're buying you must ensure that the birds are well feathered. There should be no bare patches anywhere on the body. As long as you keep the new birds separated from others, infectious illnesses shouldn't arise.
If you want to use the birds to start breeding, the first step is to decide what you want or better

still what you are capable of handling. Birds need daily care and attention, so if you're not going to have any time for them it's best not to start at all. I work with twenty or so breeding pairs, for example, which demands a little less than an hour of my time per day.

Should you decide to go ahead and breed lovebirds, find out as much as you can for yourself in advance. Visit some exhibitions and get to know a breeder.

There are also specialised lovebird societies and associations you can join.

What to look out for?

Once you know what you want to do with the birds you're planning to buy, it's time to decide which birds you want to buy. You can use the following guidelines:

- If you're looking for a tame household pet the best choice is *A. roseicollis*.
- Check that the bird you fancy is healthy. The easiest way is to look to make sure that the bird isn't sitting shaped like a ball with its feathers puffed up. You can also use you fingers to feel along the muscles either side of the breastbone. These should be firm enough for the breastbone

not to feel sharp to the touch. The bird should not be too thin.

- If you are looking for breeding birds, *A. roseicollis*, *A. fischeri* or *A. personatus* are the most suitable to begin with because they breed quite easily. In the early stages, restrict yourself to the natural colour and give yourself time to learn about inheritance. If you were to start to experiment immediately, you would almost certainly end up disappointed so it's best to leave more complex crossings to more experienced breeders for the time being.
- Don't take on too many birds. It's quality that counts, not the quantity, and you will be better off to pay a little more for a good couple than to buy two cheaper, lower quality pairs.
- Buy only young, rung birds.
- It's sometimes difficult to be sure of a bird's sex so get the breeder to agree during purchase to exchange a bird in the event you should discover that the couple is not a true pair.
- Find out when the birds were hatched and from which parents they came.
- Find out what food the young birds have been given until now. This information is very important if you are buying a young breeding bird. Some breeders put young birds into separate cages and give them the minimum of diets simply because they are going to be sold. If feed

lacks the necessary vitamins and minerals, this can lead to disappointing breeding results in the first year. I personally buy birds that are about six months old to give myself six months to feed them a balanced diet in preparation for breeding

Where to buy?

Although many breeders rear their birds well it's important for beginners to know that some don't.

Don't buy your birds just anywhere. Visit as many breeders as you can in your area so that you can quickly separate the wheat from the chaff and pay special attention to the following points:

- Accommodation and hygiene must be of the highest standard. If feed and drink dishes are seriously contaminated (with droppings or green algae) and the birds are getting little or no fresh air, it's highly likely that they will not be in their best condition.
- Inspect the bird's accommodation paying special attention to the droppings. Even though lovebirds, like all other birds, excrete faeces and urine from the same body opening (the cloaca), the droppings should not appear to be too watery. Droppings that are too watery may indicate digestion problems that result in the urine component being produced but no faeces.

A. roseicollis, dominant pied green

- It goes almost without saying that to avoid inbreeding you should not buy a pair that are related to each other. Every respectable breeder keeps a breeding register detailing which animals are related to each other.
- When you are buying an animal to introduce new blood into your aviary choose a specimen that is preferably three and half years old or more. This will reduce the risk of the newcomer passing a virus infection on to your other birds (this principally concerns 'Psittacine Beak and Feather Disease').
- Don't accept a bird that for any reason doesn't appeal to you. Don't feel obliged to buy. If you feel uncertain, take somebody with you who has a little experience in bird breeding. No respectable fancier will object.

Sexing

If you are going to keep your birds solely as pets the sex is unimportant. If you want to use the animals for breeding a sexual difference of course is a pre-requisite!
The visual differences between the cocks and the hens in lovebirds occur only in *A. pullarius*, *A. taranta* and *A. canus*.
There are no external visible differences in the remaining six species, from which a bird's sex can be determined.
Nearly every fancier has his or her own method of sexing cocks and hens. There are people who can tell the difference from the shape of the bill or the head.
I personally know fanciers that use a pendulum, but as far as I am concerned, the pelvic test is still a relatively reliable method and the most used. In this test the pelvis is examined with the index finger. In adults the entrance in hens is much wider than in cocks. Whilst this method is not one hundred percent reliable, it can give a good indication as long as the birds are sexually mature.

If sexing is unsuccessful using the method described, you can use the following trick. Place a number of unrelated birds together and provide them with sufficient nesting boxes. After a short while, pairs that form will retire to the breeding block to sleep. It's then very simple when it's dark to close the nesting boxes, remove the birds and place them in a breeding cage. You can also put all the birds in a large cage. When particular couples start keeping each other company, you can wet them with a plant sprayer and remove them. This is of course less simple when you have planned line breeding or want to produce mutations and want to pair birds on this basis. In all other cases, you can only be sure of the sex when any eggs that have been laid turn out to have been fertilised.

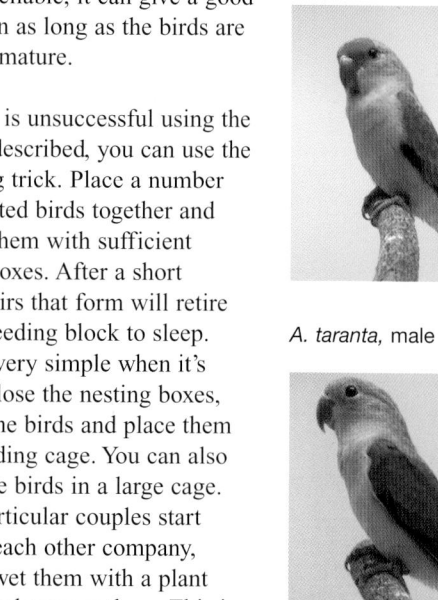

A. taranta, male

A. taranta, female

I've made mistakes sexing birds on a number of occasions in the past and it won't be the last time. Anybody who suggests the contrary is not being honest with him or herself. I had such a pair not so long ago that often kept each other company. I caught them, noted the ring numbers and separated them. When the first eggs arrived it turned out that the Palehead that I had thought was a cock was actually a hen and the Green roseicollis, that I had suspected was a hen, was in fact a cock.

The most reliable way to sex lovebirds is by endoscopic examination. Having first anaesthetised the bird the vet introduces an endoscope (a tube with a magnifying lens) through a small incision in the bird's abdominal wall into one of the air sacs to view the sex organs: the hen's ovaries have a bumpy appearance whilst the cock's testes are smooth.

Agapornis roseicollis:
edged dilute
violet turquoise

Accommo-dation

This small book assumes that you want to keep lovebirds as pets and therefore in the house. Outdoor aviaries are therefore not covered in this chapter.

Cages

A wide range of cages is available for housing lovebirds. As a general rule: the bigger the cage, the better.

When buying, make sure that you get one with horizontal bars. Lovebirds love to climb and clamber around. If the bars are vertical, that won't be possible. Equip the cage with perches of different thickness to ensure that the birds will be able to make the best use of the muscles in their toes and feet. Make sure that the cage can be cleaned easily. It's important as well that feed and water can be given without running the risk of the birds escaping. Ideally there should be enough space in the cage for a bird bath. Lovebirds like to bathe several times each day. Feed and water bowls need to be firmly anchored to something solid to ensure that they can't be tipped over or the birds injured.

Cage litter

It goes almost without saying that hygiene is one of the most important considerations when birds are housed in indoor cages. You will need to regularly remove droppings from the cage. If you use cage litter the droppings won't stick to the bottom of the cage. A good example is shell grit. You can spread this in a thin layer on the bottom of the cage but you will need to change it every three to four days. You can also use ready-to-use wood chips that are available at pet shops, amongst other places. Some people use newspaper as cage litter but I would strongly advise against it for lovebirds: the birds will tear the paper apart and eat some of it. Any printer's ink they might digest will certainly not be beneficial to their health! Problems can arise in a living room because many birds throw scraps out of the cage.

The best location

The best place in the house for caged lovebirds depends upon a number of factors. In any event, you will need to take into account the fact that these birds can sometimes make a lot of noise, which can take up all your attention. They will also throw seed out of the cage so the floor in the surrounding area needs to be easy to keep clean. The temperature in the area of the cage needs to be kept constant. Large temperature fluc-

tuations guarantee moulting problems. Ensure that the room is not constantly bathed in sunlight and that the cage isn't subjected to too much artificial light or placed in an area that's often dark. Lighting needs to be provided with regularity. If the cage area is lit one day from 7 a.m. to 6 p.m. and the following day from 6 a.m. to midnight, problems can be expected and you will end up with stressed birds and all the consequences that stress produces.

A. nigrigenis
pastel green

A. nigrigenis,
dark eyed clear

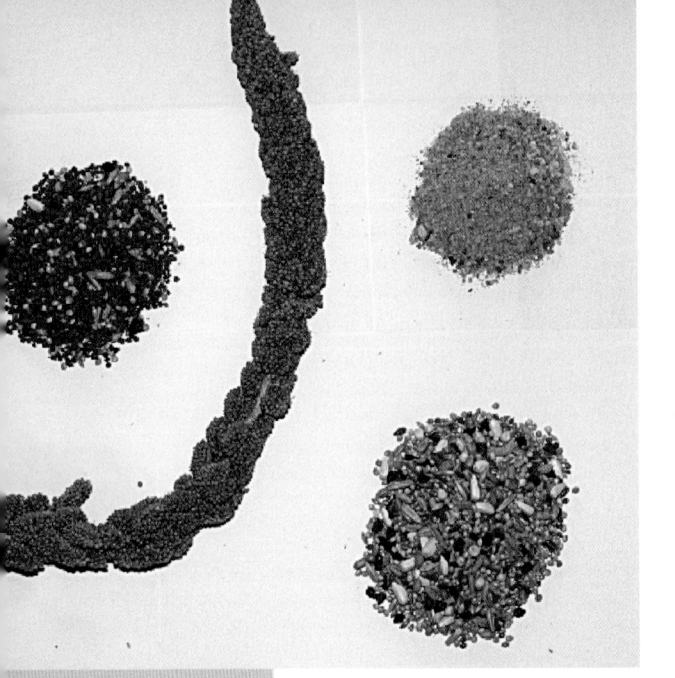

Nutrition

Nutrition is the primary requirement of every living being. Life simply cannot exist without it.

A lot of discussions take place about 'ideal' nutrition and people often undertake years or research to discover the ideal ratio of amino acids, fats, vitamins and proteins, but the fact is that the nutrition requirements differ per living being and from season to season (such as the moulting, breeding and brooding seasons). It's impossible for inexperienced individuals to mix their own lovebird feed. I even think it's time and effort wasted because there is more than enough ready-made feed available on the market.

Nutrition in the wild
Prior to man's intervention lovebirds lived exclusively in tropical areas of Africa and Madagascar. Birds in these areas still feed on seeds, fruits, berries, leaf buds, flowers, insects and larvae and, because each species has it's own feeding habits, there is little problem in the wild with competition for food. *A. pullarius* for example eats grass seeds on the ground, while *A. swindernianus* eats figs, seeds and insects high in the treetops Wild lovebirds consume more than forty different varieties of plants partially or wholly so it's an impossible task to analyse their daily intake. Even if such an analysis could be completed, it couldn't be used to define the nutritional needs of captive lovebirds because their needs differ from those of wild birds.

Seed mixes
Ready to use seed mixes are widely available in versions to suit practically every type of bird. In

general the quality of these mixes is good but the mix itself can be a problem. Lovebirds have the tendency to pick out their favourite seeds and ignore the rest. Over time, an unbalanced diet can lead to them suffering from a lack of nutrition and vitamins. You can prevent this by rationing the feed you give them to only enough for one day. In the morning they will eat the seeds they like most. Later in the day they will eat the remainder simply because there is no alternative. This way you can be sure that they receive a diet that's more or less complete.

The seeds most commonly found in mixes are: Canary seed, de-hulled oats, hemp, linseed, Panicum millet, French White millet, Japanese millet, buckwheat, whole-grain rice and whole oats. Sometimes white and striped sunflower seeds are added. More or less every fancier has his own theory about the ideal proportions. With seed mixes, take into account that the birds will be doing a lot of peeling and there will be quite a lot of husks in the feed bowl and on the ground. It's not unheard of for birds to die of starvation because an owner mistook husks for seeds so check the feed bowl carefully! Take the feed bowl in your hand and blow out the loose husks. The heavier, untouched seeds will be all that remains in the bowl.

Egg food

If you are breeding birds you will need to make a differentiation in the feed you provide. Birds raising young have specific nutritional requirements and hens, in addition to producing eggs, need to be able to manufacture enough nutrition in their crop to feed their young in the early days. This is why fanciers feed their birds egg food during the breeding season. The principle is simple: to supply protein and vitamins in an uncomplicated way. Egg food used to be home-made from dry breadcrumbs mixed with boiled egg, some extra vitamins and sometimes with a little sprouting seed. Nowadays, good quality, ready to use, egg foods are available in shops.

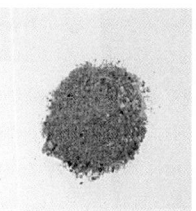

egg food

Every fancier who uses egg food has a 'secret' recipe. One mixes different egg foods together, the other adds supplements and there are those who swear by home made egg food. The latter isn't a problem at all as long as you remember moderation. A little additional vitamin won't do any harm, whereas excessive amounts of specific vitamins can be damaging to health. A good seed mix combined with a balanced egg food should in principle be more than sufficient for lovebirds. Many people unfortunately take it upon themselves to experiment, which results in there always being a little too much or a little

egg food

too little of one thing or the other. In the worst case this can cause a diet to lack the balance it needs which over a long period of time can have serious consequences for a bird's health.

Germinating seeds

Germinated seeds are a simple way of giving birds extra green feed and vitamins. The following is a typical method used. Thoroughly wash germinating seeds in cold running water and let them soak for about twelve hours changing the water four or five times. Pour the seeds into a propagating bowl and let them stand for 48 hours or so to slowly germinate. Refresh the water in the propagation bowls regularly. Finally, thoroughly rinse the seeds in cold water, let them drain and give them to the birds as extra feed mixed with a quantity of egg food. Ready to use germinating seed mixes specially formulated for lovebirds are available in shops and mostly include cardy, buckwheat, paddy rice, wheat, barley, oats, milo, dari, hemp and katjang idjoe. Some fanciers only use germinated wheat and hemp seed in the assumption that these

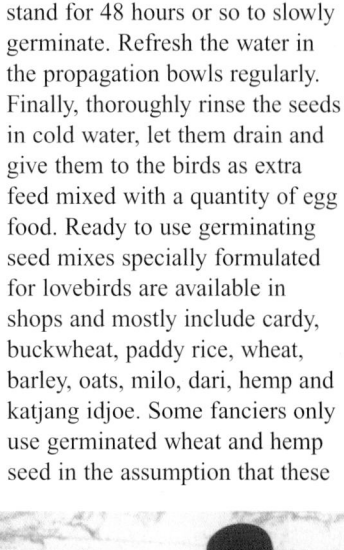

stimulate breeding but to date no firm evidence has been found to support the theory.

In many countries hemp is not used for germinating as only sterile seed is sold for bird seed as the plant produces a prohibited substance.

As I have mentioned, the ideal feed is dependent upon a number of factors. Opinion is divided but whilst it's true that germinated seeds can correct a vitamin shortage, they are not the cure-all they are sometimes claimed to be. A word of caution: any germinating seeds remaining in the cage a few hours after they have been given should be removed because they sour quite quickly.

Pellets

This method of feeding originated in the USA and also became established in Europe a few years ago. The principle is simple: all essential food elements are processed into a solution that is then baked into easily digestible pellets. Since the pellets all have the same ingredients a bird will always receive balanced nutrition without the risk of deficiencies. There are other advantages too. A specific pellet feed is available for practically every type of bird and every type of situation. This makes it unnecessary to add egg food and vitamins during the breeding season. Because pellets are generally eaten completely, wastage is kept to a minimum.

Pellets

One possible disadvantage is that birds have to adjust to eating pellets, although, once they have adjusted, problems don't normally arise. Experience has taught me that lovebirds will adjust to a change in feed with little difficulty. As with anything new though, this style of feeding has its opponents. We shouldn't forget the raised eyebrows when dry dog food was introduced 25 years ago and yet today we couldn't imagine being without it.

Extras

Everybody likes to pamper themselves and sometimes their pet(s), whether it's a dog, a goldfish or a bird. There is nothing wrong with that at all as long it's not taken to extremes and you remember that pampering is about extras.

Lovebirds for example are crazy about pieces of fruit, millet spray, half ripe maize and broccoli.

In any event make sure that any extras you give them come from natural sources (no artificial colourings etc.). Preferably no sugars or items containing sugar.

My own experience with pellets

I became acquainted with pellets in 1997. At the time I was editor of the BVA (Belgische Vereniging Agapornis, or the Belgian Lovebird Society) magazine and received an invitation from a large manufacturer of animal food to a press presentation for their latest product: pellet feed.

I was very sceptical about the new feed and had my doubts. The presentation was very persuasive, but I still couldn't imagine myself giving the feed to my birds. I had the idea that it was simply a publicity stunt that without doubt would go no further. How could anyone feed pellets to their birds?

I had naturally heard of breeding that had gone wrong and other unpleasant side effects caused by this latest discovery. For us fanciers the classic method of feeding was still the best.

A few months later, to my surprise, I heard from a friend that he had been feeding *A. lilianae* the new pellets for a while. He was clearly satisfied with the results. With a disappointing breeding season just behind me, my friend suggested that I make a new attempt using the pellets. Still not completely convinced, I obtained a 2.5 kilo (5 pounds) bag of pellets for larger parrots. We mixed them with the usual feed and waited to see what would happen.

A. lillinae

My birds naturally tossed the unfamiliar pellets out of the feed bowl. Things didn't look good and the birds were clearly not eating any of it. I contacted the manufacturer and was advised to use a feeding schedule that would provide an optimal transition to pellets. The method that the manufacturer recommended was to mix increasing amounts of the pellets in the regular feed. Well, fingers crossed.

The first step was to give the birds precisely the amount of seed that they needed for one day. Ten percent were the new pellets. Naturally, they went untouched the first day. The following day, they received eighty percent seed and twenty percent pellets. I now noticed the odd pellet being pecked left and right. Could it be that...?! The next day the birds received seventy percent seed and the remainder as pellets. To my utter amazement I saw that a couple of Fischeri were eating pellets! The amount of pellets continued to be increased until the mix consisted of twenty percent seed and eighty percent pellets.

Despite everything, I had the feeling that the birds were still too inclined to peel the pellets which was resulting in too much being wasted. A friend advised me to switch to a smaller type of pellet more suited to lovebirds. This transition went very quickly. After a couple of days the birds were eating the pellets without any problem at all, and without peeling them.

Now that the birds had been successfully moved over to the new food, it was a question of waiting to see what the breeding results would be like. With understandable doubts, I let the birds into the breeding cages. How would things work out? They hadn't had any egg food for several months and I wondered if I was doing the right thing, or if I had become the victim of a well-organised advertising stunt? The birds were offered nesting boxes in mid-October and the first results already looked promising. Nest making had started quite quickly and the first eggs had been laid within fourteen days but now the time had come, would the birds feed the pellets to

A. fischeri, blue

their young? The day after the first had hatched I took a look. To my great relief the young were still alive. Slowly but surely I became more and more convinced that the pellets really were a complete feed.

Today I still give my lovebirds a basic diet of eighty percent pellets and twenty percent seed. That doesn't mean that I don't also give them green food, spray millet and other 'treats' but I haven't provided them with egg food now for two years and breeding has not suffered as a result, in fact to the contrary. Fewer birds die now in the first few months of life and I have the impression that they moult more easily.

The subject of nutrition often comes up during the lectures I regularly give in Belgium and The Netherlands about lovebirds. When I am talking about pellets and ask for the audience's opinion, the subject produces quite a few negative reactions and stories. Further questioning reveals that few have actually tried the pellets and that the majority have formed their opinions based upon second hand information.

I understand from contacts with colleagues of the American ALBS (African Love Bird Society) that pellet feeding has been established in the United States for years. Feeding with seed is much less

common. The majority of European enthusiasts are somewhat conservative where it comes to feed. It's easy to understand. Although I had my doubts in the beginning about this new product, experimentation has convinced me of the quality of pellets and I can recommend them to all lovebird breeders. Whilst it's true that pellets are more expensive to buy, the birds eat less, waste very little and don't need egg food or extra vitamins, so I don't spend any more money on their feed per year than I did when I was feeding them with seed.

A. fischeri, double factored, edged dark green

Species

The genus of Agapornis is made up of nine species and six sub-species. At the beginning of this book, you will have seen a short summary of the members of this colourful family. In this chapter you can read more about their beautiful appearance, their origins and their special characteristics.

A. taranta, male

Agapornis taranta

There are two known types of *A. taranta*: the main species *A. taranta taranta* and the sub-species *A. taranta nana*. In English, fanciers talk of the Abyssinian lovebird, in French of psittacule à masque rouge, in German of Tarantapapagei or Taranta Unzertrennlicher and in Dutch of Abessijnse agapornis or bergpapegaai. The bird was given its Latin name by Sir Henry Stanley.

A. taranta was discovered in Northeast Africa in 1814. The main species, *A. taranta taranta* originated in mid and eastern Ethiopia and in southern Eritrea. Stanley named the species after a mountain pass in Ethiopia. Taranta's are mountain birds that

live at heights of between 4,000 and 6,500 feet (1300 and 2000 meters). Because they are acclimatised to high altitudes the birds are well able to cope with low night-time temperatures. Due to tightened import restrictions applying to rare animals, Taranta's are no longer imported from the wild. Animals bred in captivity though are readily available.

Description

At 6.5 inches (16.5 centimetres) *A. taranta* is the largest member of the Agapornis family. The cock has a typical red brow and red rings around the eyes. The large flight feathers are black and the wing edges from the bend in the wing are blue/black. The coverts are black, a characteristic found in all three of the sexually

Species

In the wild

In the wild, Taranta's live in small groups resting at night in tree hollows. In the breeding season the hen makes a shallow bowl-like bed of twigs, branches and leaf. This nesting material is collected and transported by the hen in her body plumage, a method of transport typical of the sexually dimorphic group and for *A. roseicollis*. What is unique is that the hen sheds part of her breast and belly plumage shortly before laying her eggs, possibly plucking them out herself, to use them as a lining in the nest hollow. This behaviour is absent in all other *Agapornis*. The hen will then lay an egg every other day totalling between three and six eggs. The first eggs hatch after a brooding period of about

A. taranta, male

A. taranta
Upper left: female,
lower right: male

dimorphic group. The tail bears a black ring at the rearmost edge. The beak is red, the iris brown and the toes and feet are dark grey. The remainder of the body is green. The hen lacks the red brow and the blue/black wing edges. The undersides of the wings are green/grey, but she is otherwise identical to the cock.

Sub-species

The sub-species *A. taranta nana* was discovered in the north of Ethiopia and described by Neumann in 1931. This sub-species differs by nature of its shorter wings and a smaller bill. The *taranta nana* in addition produces more eggs in a year than the nominate race.

25 days. The hatchlings are covered with white down which changes to grey and then green, as they get older. The young leave the nest after fifty days. In the wild, they mostly eat grass seeds, berries and fruit. They also like ripe figs.

Buying

Because Taranta's are still quite expensive, I would advise against buying them until they are about nine months old and their colour has fully developed. This way you will not run the risk of buying two cocks or that they will die during the first moult. The taranta is the only Agapornid species that takes two years to become sexually mature. There is therefore no reason to rush into buying but, when you do, pay special attention to the shape and colour of the nails. Specimens that are not up to standard are definitely not a suitable basis upon which to build your stock.

Exhibition bird

The taranta is highly suitable for exhibitions. Thanks to their docile character they can easily be trained with a little patience. I know a number of fanciers who have a tame taranta in their collection. Taranta's however are seldom kept as domestic pets, possibly due to the high purchase price.

Mutations

Over time, a number of different taranta mutations have appeared, of which the dark factor is such that dark green and double dark green birds now appear in addition to green. Despite the fact that these mutations are still quite expensive they can often be found in breeder collections. So-called fallow mutations came from Germany. In this mutation, the black eumelanin colour appears grey. This produces a bird that is somewhat duller in colour, with grey flight feathers. This mutation also prevents darker colours from forming in the feet and eyes whereby the fallow retains its typical red eyes and flesh coloured feet. This mutation is called recessive.

I have recently seen cinnamon and lutino mutations for the first time. These were in their early stages and consequently very weak. The lutinos died after a few days. Of the cinnamon mutants only one survived. Experimental breeding therefore could take place. References to this lutino mutation can be found in print, as can references to the blue mutation that occurs in Portugal. Despite intensive investigation carried out by a number of local contacts, this mutation has not been sighted. Since 2002 misty is added to the taranta mutations.

Agapornis pullarius

A. pullarius also appears in two sub-species: *A. pullarius pullarius* and the sub-species *A. p.ugandae*. This species is called the Red-faced Lovebird. The *pullarius* were discovered in equatorial west and central Africa.

Description

The pullarius is approximately 6 inches (15 centimetres) in length. The forehead and cheeks of the adult cock are orange/red. The body is predominantly green. The breast, belly, flanks and vent exhibit a yellowish flush. The mantle is green. The upper wing covering is green and gives the impression of having a hammer finish. The wing edges of the cocks from the bend in the wing consist of a mixture of dark ultramarine blue and a few sky blue feathers. The under wing coverts are black. The large flight feathers are dark grey to black. The rump is sky blue. The upper tail covert feathers are green. The underside tail covert feathers are a yellowish green. The large tail feathers that are practically covered by the upper and lower tail covert feathers display a red, yellow, black band pattern. The tips of the tail are green. The beak is tomato red. The rings around the eyes are each made up of a narrow band of small white and blue feathers. The eyes are dark brown. The feet are grey and the nails are dark grey. The hen's forehead, head, cheeks and the neck are a pale orange red and she lacks the blue and dark ultramarine blue wing edges. The wing edges of the hen are coloured green/yellow. The lower wing covert feathers are green.

A. pullarius, young

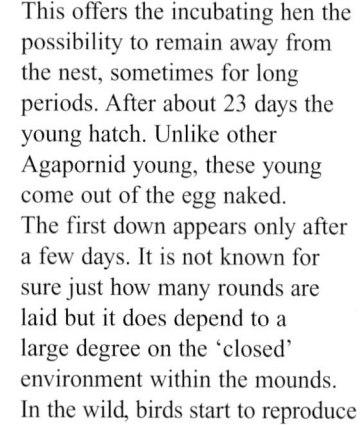

Sub-species
In addition to *A. pullarius pullarius* there is the sub-species *A. pullarius ugandae*. As the name implies, this sub-species is only found in the wild in Uganda. It differs in one respect only from the nominate species, namely because of the paler blue colour of the rump.

In the wild

The Pullarius lives in groups of between twenty and thirty birds in sparsely wooded savannah where they feed mainly on grass seed that is readily available. The wide space of the savannahs is also home to their nesting places. Unlike other lovebirds the pullarius nests in termite mounds and not in tree hollows. The termites construct these mounds with a mixture of saliva, wood and sand. The carton like constructions can reach heights of 20 feet (6 metres) and can be found in trees as well as on the ground.

The hen excavates a passage into a mound terminating it in a nesting chamber. Eggs are laid every other day. Strangely enough, the termites, which are very aggressive towards invaders, leave the pullarius undisturbed. This is probably because the pullarius only uses parts of the mound not inhabited by the termites. Some sources say that that the pullarius also likes to eat termites. Given the aggressive nature of these insects, however, this would seem somewhat unlikely.

The main advantage of termite mounds is that their core temperature is nearly always constant. This offers the incubating hen the possibility to remain away from the nest, sometimes for long periods. After about 23 days the young hatch. Unlike other Agapornid young, these young come out of the egg naked. The first down appears only after a few days. It is not known for sure just how many rounds are laid but it does depend to a large degree on the 'closed' environment within the mounds. In the wild, birds start to reproduce when the breeding conditions are optimal: sufficient food, good nesting facilities, ideal temperatures sufficient daylight and so on. It's unlikely that more than two rounds will be raised in the wild.

Mutations
The existence of a lutino Red-faced in Portugal is cited in Messrs. Brockmann and Lantermann's book "The World of Lovebirds". Jim Hayward described a blue specimen in 1979. Hard evidence that these mutants existed though has not been forthcoming. If they did exist then in all likelihood they will not have been bred in captivity because the number of successfully bred pullarius can be counted on one hand.

Agapornis canus

The canus is the third and last of the sexually dimorphic group in which colour differences exist between cocks and hens. The nominate species *A. canus canus* has a sub-species, *A. canus ablectanae*. The canus is found in the coastal areas of the Malagasy Republic (formally Madagascar) and was described for the first time in 1788. *A. canus* is a member of the genus of Agapornis and is considered a form that is transitional to the Loricules (another family of dwarf parrots).

Description

A. canus is approximately 5,5 inches long (14 centimetres). The cock has a typical pearl-grey head, neck and breast. The body is green. The hen is almost completely green. Apart from the specific colour differences, all cocks possess black under wing coverts. In hens these are green.

Sub-species

The only known sub-species of *A. canus canus* was discovered and described in 1918. The *A. canus ablectanae* male has a deeper grey coloured and violet suffused head, neck and breast. The general body colour is a darker green. The hen, just like the cock, is a little darker in colour. It is unlikely that this difference is to be found in birds bred in captivity.

In the wild

The canus is to be found in open wooded areas on slopes along coastlines. They are gregarious and feed exclusively on grass seeds. Although they live in large groups, they cannot be considered colony animals because in the breeding season couples mostly split away from the rest of the group. These birds nest in holes in trees where the hen uses pieces of wood and grass as nesting material, transporting them between the feathers of the body, breast and rump.

In captivity

Madagascars are generally considered difficult to breed in captivity. Nevertheless, some breeders manage successfully to produce

A. canus, male

A. canus, female

and raise a number of nests and are involved in pioneering canus breeding work.

It's difficult to provide fixed rules for successful breeding. Every fancier does it in his or her own way. One uses an ordinary nesting box for lovebirds with a turf cage litter. Another has a deep budgerigar nesting box with coconut fibre nesting material. Some breeders use laurel leaves in the nest, others don't use any nesting material at all. It's simply a question of experimentation and watching to see how things turn out. Three things are essential when breeding the canus. Money: to buy the birds. Patience: while waiting for the results and, luck. The canus is only sporadically available in bird shops and it's therefore of great importance that fanciers do everything possible to expand the stock of domesticated birds.

Mutations
Until today there are no known *A. canus* mutations. A yellow specimen however can be found in America.

In this case it's a hen that emerged green from the egg and transformed completely in time to yellow. Whether the transformation has been caused by a mutation or a abnormality in the plumage is not certain because until now the bird has not produced any young. The fact that the hen was the normal green colour at birth in this case may indicate an abnormality or a modification (mutations continue to be inherited, abnormalities and modifications are not).

Agapornis roseicollis
The roseicollis is considered to be an intermediate form between the sexually dimorphic and the white eye-ring group (the Personata group). This species was discovered in 1793 in south-west Africa. Scientists at first thought it was the sub-species of *A. pullarius* but it was recognised as an independent species in 1817. The nominate species *A. roseicollis roseicollis* possesses a sub-species: *A. roseicollis catumbella*.

Description
The roseicollis is about 6 inches (16 cm) in length and mainly green. The face is peach coloured, dark red at the crown reducing to a deep rose colour under the bill. The rump is blue. The bill is horn coloured, the feet are grey and the nails dark grey to black.

Sub-species
The sub-species *A. roseicollis catumbella* is smaller in size but more intensely coloured, and its bill has a pinkish tinge. It is otherwise the same as the nominate species. This bird was only described and recognised as a sub-species in 1955.

In the wild
In the wild the roseicollis live in flights of twenty to thirty birds.

Agapornis roseicollis, edged dilute green

Agapornis roseicollis, dominant pied violet turquoise

They often use the nests of the Weaverbird to breed in. The weavers (small birds that live in the same habitat as the roseicollis and make ball shaped nests) make communal nests containing anywhere between ten and one hundred or more nesting spaces. The roseicollis will chase off the rightful occupants and take over a part of their nest spaces. Roseicollis don't add new nesting material to these ready-to-use nests as they do when they make use of holes in trees or buildings. The way that nesting materials are collected is unique to the roseicollis: the hen will stick small pieces of bark or twigs between the rump and upper tail feathers. Strangely enough, she doesn't bother to recover any material that she drops.

Mutations

The roseicollis is the Agapornis species in which the most mutations have appeared. In addition to the dark factors and the violet factor, there are aqua, ino, orange face, turquoise, edged dilute, suffused, bronze fallow, pale fallow, cinnamon, pallid, pale headed, recessive pied, dominant pied. Since the end of the '90s we also recognise an opaline mutation. A truly blue roseicollis has not materialised to date. Many of the above mutations can be combined, which can lead to attractive results but also to a cacophony of colours that can create misunderstanding and confusion. Leave experimen-

tation for the time being to experienced fanciers because there is a limit to the combinations accepted at exhibitions. Remember one golden rule in any event: a combination in which the mutations are not clearly recognisable is neither suitable as an exhibition bird nor as a breeding bird. Such combinations only create confusion that serves nobody's interests.

Lesser known was the long feathered *roseicollis Roseicollis* that are much stockier than the original wild species. These have recently become the exhibition standard in Europe. These birds have a bright red coloured face and an almost colourless bill. Their legs are often too thick for the standard 4.5 mm ring and have to be ringed with a large 5 mm ring.

When these primarily Dutch-bred birds were first shown in The Netherlands, the usual discussions and rumours started to spread. The birds were big because they were fed some secret potion; they were given hormones. Others said that they were crossed with the sub-species catumbella. Even inside the COM (Commitee Ornithologic Mondual), some countries were of the same opinion.

The truth is actually much simpler: these birds were (just like the standard budgerigar) the result of careful selection. Jac de Jong of

A. roseicollis,
opaline pallid
dark green

A. roseicollis, orange geaded, pallid green

the Netherlands was one of the pioneers in the area of breeding these long feathered birds. The discussion as to their authenticity continues even today in countries where these long-feathered birds appear for the first time (such as the United States). A repetitive factor in these discussions is that non-owners voice negative theories, whereas owners are enthusiastic and proud. I was confronted with an example of a negative attitude regarding these birds a short while ago: the "too red face' of the long-feathered birds is the result of crossing with *A. fischeri.* When I reminded the person involved that the result of such a crossing would be infertile I received the following surprising answer: "Yes, possibly the first generation,

A. roseicollis, green

but maybe they will become fertile by the third generation!" I asked if he could explain how that would be possible: my grandfather was infertile, my father as well, but luckily enough I wasn't. He couldn't give me a reply...

It looks as though the majority of fanciers, wherever they are in the world, are very suspicious when confronted something new, and for them unknown. The easiest way of dealing with such a situation is to dismiss out of hand anything they don't have themselves. That's peculiar because, at the same time, many of the same people are making frantic attempts to obtain a pair of 'false' birds. The standard (English) budgerigars, when first seen, were greeted with loud enthusiasm. Now, when the same thing happens to Roseicollis, everybody suddenly sees ghosts. Maybe it's just a little jealousy?

Agapornis swindernianus

The fact that it has never been exported to our parts means that very little is known about this bird. One of the possible reasons is its food: this bird lives mainly on seeds and figs that grow exclusively in its original habitat. On top of that it lives in virtually impenetrable jungle. The description of this species and of its subspecies that follow were written by H.W.J. van der Linden, a well-known Dutch ornithologist. The nominate species *A. swinder-*

nianus swindernianus is a small representative of the family of Agapornis discovered in 1820 by Kuhl and named after Professor Th. van Swinderen. The sub-species *A. swindernianus zenkeri*, was discovered in 1895 and named after its discoverer G. Zenker. The other sub-species, *A. swindernianus emini* were given the Christian name of German traveller and explorer Emin Pascha. in 1908.

A. swindernianus swindernianus
Length: 13 cm
Cock and hen: The forehead, top of the skull and the back of the head are grass green. The cheeks and bib are more of a yellowish green. The general body colour is green, the breast, belly and anal area somewhat paler. There is a characteristic short black band on the back of the neck that becomes a yellow collar around the entire neck. The upper wing, the mantel and the underwing coverts are green. The large flight feathers are black. The rump and upper tail covert feathers are purple/blue, the underside tail covert feathers are a yellowish green. The large tail feathers that are practically covered by the upper and lower tail coverts display a red and black diagonal marking from the base that transforms into green at the tips. The eyes are brown with a clear yellow iris. The bill is anthracite coloured. The legs are a greenish dark grey and the nails dark grey.
Young: The black neck ring is not present. The bill is light grey with a black patch on the upper bill.
Eggs: Thought to be white. Number unknown.
Distribution: Liberia

A. swindernianus zenkeri
Cock and hen: The collar around the neck is red/brown extending to the upper breast from where it gradually transforms into a blue/green colour on the lower breast. This sub-species is otherwise the same as the nominate species.
Distribution: Cameroon, eastern Gabon and the western part of the Central African Republic and the Congo.

A. swindernianus emini
Cock and hen: The red/brown collar around the neck is much less extensive and does not extend to the upper breast. The bill is much more strongly bent. Otherwise the same as *A. swindernianus zenkeri*.
Distribution: The eastern part of the Congo, to deep into west Uganda.

Agapornis personatus
This Agapornis species was discovered in 1887 in north-east Tanzania. It's territory lies only some sixty kilometres south-east of the range of Fischer's lovebird.

Agapornis roseicollis, double dark aqua

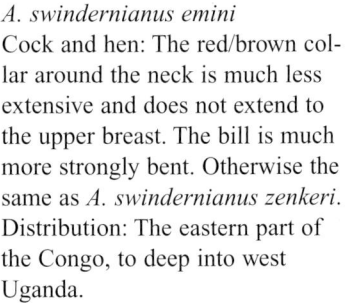

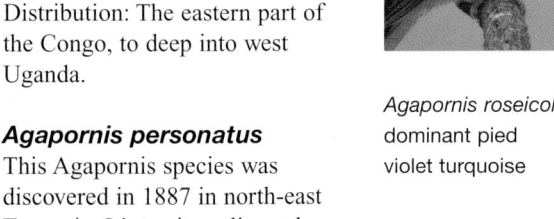

Agapornis roseicollis, dominant pied violet turquoise

Description

The wild form of *A. personatus* has a deep black head. A yellow collar extends from the back of the neck to the breast. A typical white eye-ring surrounds each of the brown eyes. The dominant body colour is green, the bend of the wing is yellow and the rump dark blue on a greenish base. The bill is deep coral red. The feet are grey and the claws are black. There is no visible difference between the cock and the hen.

In the wild

The habitat of the personatus is lightly wooded savannah, grassland with a few scattered trees and bushes. Their food consists of a variety of readily available seeds and berries. The personatus make its nests in tree cavities. Like all lovebirds they lay their eggs on alternate days and brood for approximately 23 days.

Buying

A young personatus is particularly susceptible to stress. Do not therefore buy very young birds or you will run the risk of them dying within a few days. It's better to wait until the animals are 10 months old or so.

Mutations

A relatively large number of mutations have occurred in the personatus. To date these are the dark factors, the blue factor, the violet factor, the pastel factor and,

not so long ago in America, fallow. The ino factor was introduced via the *lilianae* and the edged birds were produced via the *fischeri*.

Agapornis fischeri

Agapornis p.fischeri was discovered by Dr Fischer in northern Tanzania in about 1887. Small flocks of these birds are found in an area south of Lake Victoria, not far from the personatus. Their habitat consists mainly of dry savannah where they feed on grass seed. The fischeri's are also regular visitors to the local millet and maize fields. Reichenow, a publicist expert on lovebirds, named these after their discoverer. The *fischeri*, the *roseicollis* and the *personatus* are today's most popular lovebirds.

Description

The fischeri is about 6 inches (15 cm) long. The forehead is orange red reducing to a lighter tint under the bill. From the top of the head down the back, this becomes suffused with an olive green/bronze colour. Bare eye rings are found around the eyes. The main body colour is green, the bends in wing are yellow. The bill is coral red, the rump is violet coloured. The legs are grey and the nails are dark grey.

Mutations

Fischeri also have a number of colour mutations. Particular muta-

A. personatus, green

A. personatus, mauve

A. personatus, violet

tions are the dark-eyed clear, the edged and the pied birds. As far as is known, at least three forms of pied bird exist, recessive pied, dominant pied and a mottle form. The blue factor, the violet factor and the dark factors came from crossing with the *personatus*. The ino factor came from the *lilianae*.

A slate blue like fischeri was born in The Netherlands in 1998. Initially it was thought to be a slate form, but the mutation turned out to be inherited dominant. The BVA had the plumage structure of this mutant examined. Preliminary results concluded that it was neither a slate form nor was it a grey mutation. Further examination has shown that it is a slaty mutation.

Buying

The wild form of fischeri is well suited to the beginner. It is undemanding and breeding results normally appear quite quickly. Having said that, the following points are important: the size of the birds and the appearance of the mask, which must not show any dark deposits. The rump must be completely violet. A standard requirement is that the mask be as orange/red as possible and without a yellow transition area on the breast. You need to ensure that the back of the head retains a nice dark colour. I have seen a number of birds at exhibitions that have

received a high score from the judge, despite the fact that the back of the head was nearly completely red. In my view this is definitely not correct, and should as such be penalised.

If you want to begin breeding blue or other coloured fischeri anyway, it's advisable to seek the advice of more experienced breeders first. This way you will avoid breeding illegitimates from the beginning. It can't be emphasised enough: don't buy from the first breeder you come across! To buy good birds, you need to take your time. Remember that poor quality birds eat just as much as good birds, but that good quality birds are essential if you want to build up a good stock. If you should acquire a number of mutants, always cross them in the first instance with a good racially pure wild form The following year you can continue with the split-young. Stock building will take a little longer this way but the results will be far better!

Agapornis nigrigenis

Dr. Kirkman discovered this species in south-west Zambia in 1904. *A. nigrigenis* live in a relatively small area of land between the Zambezi river in the south and the Kafue river in the north. Their habitat today occupies only about 965 square miles (2500 square kilometres).

A. personatus, violet

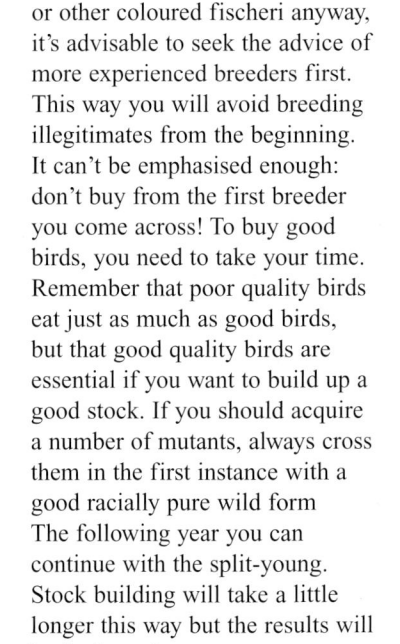

A. fischeri, double factored, edged, dark green

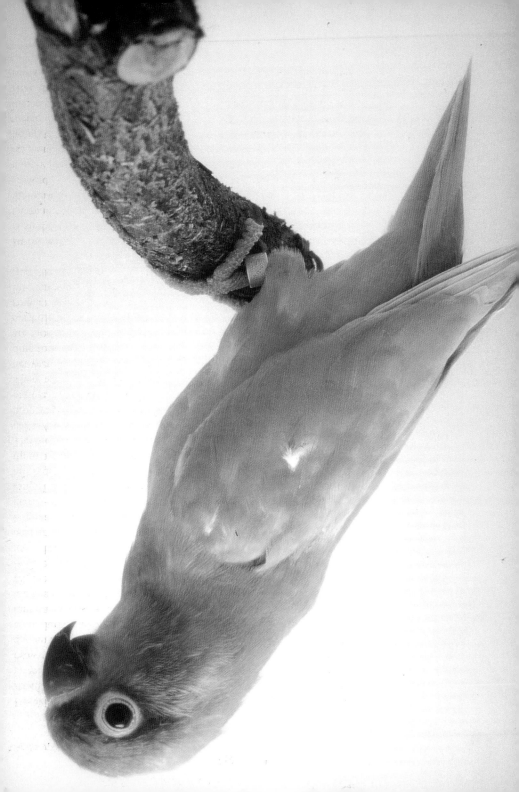

Description

At 13.5 centimetres *A. nigrigenis* is one of the smaller species. The brownish-black forehead and head darken into a dark brown. The chin, throat and cheeks are black (anthracite coloured), the back of the head is olive green. The mantel, the top of the wings and the tail are a dull grass green, the lower breast, belly, flanks and anal area are a yellowish green. The large tail feathers display an orange/red-yellow/black diagonal marking. The tail tips are green. The bill fades from bright red at the tip to a pinkish white at its base. The feet are greyish with brown nails. A white ring surrounds the brown eyes and the bird has an orange/salmon coloured bib. There are no visible differences between the sexes; even if, according to some breeders, the hens are more robust and have a broader bill base. The Nigrigenis is smaller than Personatus and Fischeri and has a typical posture (just like the lilianae).

In the wild

A study carried out by the German doctor and amateur-ornithologist Dr. W. Gilges in 1974 showed the Nigrigenis to be found mainly in the wooded areas along the Zambezi river. These woods lining the river are only a few meters deep transforming at the inland edge into dry savannah. Here the birds search for food: seeds, berries, fruit and leaf buds.

They use the riverside woods for cover and holes and cracks in the trees serve as nests. The river offers them the opportunity to bathe, something they appear to love doing.

The population seem to have survived the large-scale export of the '30s less well than it was originally thought. This is the reason why the wild Nigrigenis today is an endangered species. How this happened precisely is still a puzzle but the main cause could be the extensive changes that have taken place in their habitat: due to expanding agriculture, increasing deforestation and the reduction in watering places. With less and less millet being cultivated, finding food is becoming a problem. In addition, birds are hunted to protect the crops and to supply stock for the illegal trade in birds. It's also not unthinkable that one sickness or another might have destroyed part of the population. For this reason, Professor Mike Perrin and Louise Wilburton from the Research Centre for African Parrot Conservation at the University of Natal in Pietermaritzburg, South Africa have started a project to study and protect the Nigrigenis in its original habitat.

As mentioned, Nigrigenis were exported in large numbers in the '30s. The birds were sold for next to nothing making them uninteresting for the majority of com-

mercial breeders. As a result, they more or less lost their popularity. Luckily today, The Netherlands and Belgium, unlike other countries, are producing a large stock of birds from captive breeding. Because of this, the Nigrigenis is considered a rare species in the United States. A breeding program was even started in Germany recently for Lilianae and Nigrigenis in the hope of being able to maintain the level of the captive population.

Mutations
In all probability, only two racially pure mutations of the Nigrigenis exist at this time: the suffused mutant and the misty mutant. In the case of the suffused mutant, the melanin has disappeared from the feathers to a large degree with the result that the bird has become a dirty yellow colour. In the case of the misty mutant, the melanin has disappeared to a lesser degree producing a dull grey/green bird. The suffused mutation originated in Denmark where somebody bought four specimens from a local dealer some ten years or so ago. Of the four birds that were bought, two were sold to Brazil where both died. The remaining two ended up with Koos Hammer in The Netherlands. He had somewhat better luck in being able to keep at least one alive. A couple of tense years passed before the recessive mutant produced the first suffused young. This

breeder has now produced a number of suffused specimens, even in the blue series. Portugal produced the dark-eyed clear Nigrigenis at the end of the 90's. Whether this is a pure mutation or a transmutation we will never know, but the fact remains that it's a fine bird. The dark factors, the blue factor and the ino factor also came from transmutation with other lovebirds. In other words: the mutation was introduced by crossing another member of the group with a white eye-ring.

Maintain a respect for pure wild species and don't be blinded by attractive (trans) mutations. The nigrigenis is after all an endangered species. In any event, good (trans) mutations would not be possible were it not for the pure wild species. It's my belief that this can only be achieved through open dialog, cooperation, having respect for the opinion of others and honesty.

Agapornis lilianae
This beautiful lovebird was first described in 1864. Originally thought to be a sub-species of the Peach-faced lovebird, it wasn't until 1894 that Shelly classified them as a distinct species. He named them Agaporis *personata lilianae* after Lilian Slater, the sister of the famous ornithologist W.L. Slater. Imported into Europe in 1926, the first breeding successes soon followed in England.

Description

The lilianae is approximately 5 inches (13 cm) long. The head is bright orange/red, transforming into a slightly lighter colour on the bib. The back of the head is yellowish green transforming into olive green and on to green. The body is green. The bill is coral red changing to a pinkish white at the base with a bluish tint. The eyes are light brown with generally a lighter iris and a white ring around each eye. The legs are grey and the nails black. The lilianae has a proud posture that is more 'aristocratic' than that of the personatus or the fischeri.

A. lilianae

In the wild

In the wild, lilianae can be found in southern Tanzania, northern Zimbabwe and eastern Zambia. The birds there live close to rivers because they like to bathe a couple of times a day. The lilianae live in colonies, often of more than one hundred animals, and eat mainly grass seed and fruit. Imported birds are only sporadically traded these days.

Mutations

The lutino is the only known lilianae mutant. This autosomal recessive mutation came about in 1936 in Adelaide (Australia) at the breeding establishment of a Mr. Prendergast. It is also the ino factor of the lilianae that was transferred to the personatus and later to the fischeri. It's doubtful whether many 'real' lutino lilianae remain today. The Australian Love Bird Society let it be known a short while ago that lutino young of this recessive mutant type are born once in a while, but that they are mostly so weak that they never leave the nest. The number of living lutinos must therefore be very limited. The ALBS also reported that a couple of pastel lilianae were offered to a local dealer in Ausburn City. A certain Mr Brush is supposed to have bought them to carry out trial breeding. Further information is lacking. Whichever way you look at it the lilianae have the same mutation potential, in principle, as the other Agapornis. The fact that they are less easy to breed makes the likelihood of spontaneous mutations considerably smaller.

Sickness and health

The space in this book is too limited to be able to go in great detail into the medical to's and fro's concerning lovebirds. This chapter is therefore limited to the main issues that concern your bird's health, sicknesses and especially how you can prevent them.

A. personatus, blue

Risks

When a single bird or a couple or birds are kept as caged birds the risk of infection is quite small. You do however need to ensure that they receive the right nutrition. Over a period of time an unbalanced or incorrect diet can lead to sickness and even death (see chapter Feeding).

Viruses, bacteria, parasites and fungal infections go hand in hand with keeping a variety of lovebirds in an aviary possibly with other parrots. The risks increase if you are taking part in exhibitions or regularly buy new birds.

Prevention

There are a number of preventative steps you can take to prevent sickness. In the first place you should try where possible to limit

taking on new birds to the minimum. Obtain new birds only from reliable breeders and avoid buying new blood from shows or special bird markets.

Expose your birds to as little stress as possible. You can do this by transporting as quickly, calmly and as little as possible, while ensuring that sufficient feed and drinking water are always available to them. Give anybody minding them for you during your vacations clear instructions as to what to do!

Check their cages regularly for lice and mites. These parasites can create considerable unrest and, over a long period of time, can weaken a bird's immune system.

It's better not to house other varieties of birds together with your lovebirds, Some varieties, especially budgerigars, may carry sicknesses without actually displaying symptoms and may infect other parrots when they come into contact with them! Lovebirds in general are susceptible to infection and in most cases will get sick.

In the context of infectious sicknesses coming from other birds, you also need to ensure that wild birds and chickens are not able to access the aviary and that droppings can't fall inside.

It goes almost without saying that you need to clean your aviary on a regular basis. If you want to effectively remove the sources of infection, cleaning will need to be done in various phases:
1. With a dry brush, first remove as much loose material (droppings, straw, seed husks and other organic material) as possible.

A. fischeri,
recessive pied blue

A. nigrigenis, green

2. Clean all remaining contaminated surfaces with a brush or sponge, water and if necessary soap. Try to ensure that no traces of dirt or dust remain. Do not use a high-pressure spray! This will only spread the dirt in every direction, potentially spreading sources of infection throughout the aviary.
3. Clean all surfaces with a disinfectant solution. Bleach is cheap and efficient against many sources of infection, just as long as dirt has first been thoroughly removed.

When using very strong disinfectants you must wear protective clothing. Also don't forget to rinse and thoroughly ventilate the aviary when you're finished. These solutions are corrosive and volatile and they can cause serious foot and airway infections.

If you get the impression that your birds are sick it's not a good idea to do the doctoring yourself. It takes a professional to effectively cure sicknesses and disorders so it's best to call a vet. He or she can save your birds a lot of suffering.

Zoonotic infections
Zoonotic infections are disorders that can be passed from animals to people. These sicknesses also occur in parrots such as tuberculosis and psittacosis. A number of symptoms may indicate that your birds are troubled by disorders: breathing difficulties, continual,

unexplainable weight loss leading to death and sudden death itself. In such cases, it's advisable to consult your vet as quickly as possible. He or she will be able to confirm the cause and if necessary refer you to your own doctor. It's important to know that Zoonotic infections exist but there is no reason to panic. As long as you take hygiene seriously, the risks will be minimal.

A. personatus, green

Various

Some interesting details not yet covered in the book are mentioned in this chapter.

A. roseicollis, ino aqua and aqua

Daily care

I advise anybody who can't make the time available on a daily basis to care for his or her lovebirds not to buy the birds in the first place. Even if you only have one tame specimen, you need to devote some time to it each day. In the first place you have to provide fresh feed and drinking water daily. During the breeding season it's advisable to check the nests at least once a day. You must also clean the cage(s) thoroughly once a week.

Taming

Taming a dwarf parrot isn't as easy as falling off a log. A prerequisite is that you begin with a very young specimen. Choose a bird preferably that has just left the nest even if you need to feed it

with a syringe for a while. Ready-to-use preparations are available. Put the feed in the syringe, gently open the bird's beak and slowly inject some of the feed. The young bird will quickly get the hang of things and often take the syringe in its bill spontaneously from the second day. Food is food after all!

You will need lots of patience to get the bird used to you being around, and you will only be successful if you are relaxed yourself. Use the system of reward. If you give the bird something extra when it comes to you without you having prompted it, it will quickly establish a link and come to you regularly to collect 'treats'. Give it time to get to know its surroundings. If it doesn't come to you immediately when it's flying around the room, don't start chasing after it with a lot of noise and exaggerated movements, this will only frighten it. It's far better to lure a bird to you with a treat or, failing that, to calmly catch it in a butterfly type net. Generally speaking though, if you put something enticing into it's cage it will return to the cage on its' own.

You can be sure that you will receive a lot of pleasure from a tame lovebird but take care: some can behave as aggressively as large parrots; attacking those they are not familiar with. Lovebirds sometimes bond so strongly with an individual that all others are considered invaders and are physi-cally attacked. If you also want a talking specimen then I'm going to have to disappoint you. To date I have not come across a single talking lovebird.

The law

The number of endangered species has increased over the last decades. To provide a degree of protection against overexploitation of endangered animals (and also for plants) on an international level, the Washington Convention was brought into being in 1973 under the name CITES (Convention on International Trade in Endangered Species of Wild Fauna and Flora). This treaty of Washington was converted into uniform regulation applicable to

A. fischeri,
recesive pied green

A. roseicollis

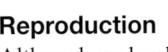

all countries belonging to the European Union effective June 1st, 1997, dividing up threatened animal and plant species into four lists according to the degree to which they are threatened. Agapornis are included in the B-list, which is broadly similar to appendix II of the Washington Convention. Appendix I (the A-list) details species that face immediate threat of extinction and may not therefore be imported or exported. The species included in the B-list, whilst not actually being in immediate danger of extinction, would be in danger if no steps were to be taken to protect them. Strict conditions apply and these species may only be captured in the wild under controlled conditions. They may only be imported with the permission of the ministries responsible.

The table below shows how species of animals are classified under the Washington Convention. The example is *A. fischeri*, the most imported parrot species in the world.

The importance of this legislation for lovebird keepers and breeders lies in the fact that the governments apply the described list to regulate ownership, import and to enforce trading bans in the species involved. Exemptions are made if you can prove without reasonable doubt that the birds in your possession have not come from the wild. Luckily, this is almost always the case. It's advisable however to check the facts yourself with your local authority to ensure that you are complying with the law. Local authority regulations may for example limit the number of birds that may be kept.

Reproduction

Although no book about Lovebirds is actually complete unless it includes information on their reproduction there is insufficient space for the subject to be covered to the degree that it deserves in this publication. Extensive information about breeding Lovebirds can be found however in Dirk van den Abeele's book Breeding Lovebirds, also planned for publication in the About Pets series.

A. fischeri,
dominant pied green

Class	:	AVES
Order	:	PSITTACIFORMES
Family	:	PSITTACIDAE
Species	:	*Agapornis fischeri*
Common	:	Fischer's Lovebird
Distribution	:	Burundi, Kenya [int], Rwanda, Tanzania
Appendix	:	II
Country	:	
Date listed	:	(06/06/1981)
Notes	:	

Other books from About Pets

Key features of the series are:
- Most affordable books
- Packed with hands-on information
- Well written by experts
- Easy to understand language
- Full colour original photography
- 70 to 110 photos
- All one needs to know to care well for their pet
- Trusted authors, veterinary consultants, breed and species expert authorities
- Appropriate for first time pet owners
- Interesting detailed information for pet professionals
- Title range includes books for advanced pet owners and breeders
- Includes useful addresses, veterinary data, breed standards.

- The Border Collie
- The Boxer
- The Cavalier King Charles Spaniel
- The Cocker Spaniel
- The Dalmatian
- The Dobermann
- The German Shepherd
- The Golden Retriever
- The Jack Russell Terrier
- The Labrador Retriever
- The Puppy
- The Rottweiler
- The Budgerigar
- The Canary
- The Cockatiel
- The Parrot
- The Cat
- The Kitten
- The Dwarf Hamster
- The Dwarf Rabbit
- The Ferret
- The Gerbil
- The Guinea Pig
- The Hamster
- The Mouse
- The Rabbit
- The Rat
- The Goldfish
- The Tropical Fish
- The Snake

Useful addresses

Becoming a member of a bird society or breeder club can be very useful for good advice and interesting activities.

Lovebird Society England

The Lovebird (1990) Society was founded as a specialist Society for Lovebird enthusiasts in December 1989, with the support of many leading breeders and exhibitors. The "(1990)" was incorporated into the name to distinguish the Society from a lovebird society that had previously existed in the UK.

It concerns itself solely with birds of the genus "Agapornis". Members range from individuals with one or two "pet" birds to large scale breeders and exhibitors and in all parts of Great Britain, including Northern Ireland and the Channel Isles, with a small but significant number of overseas members.

The Society membership is currently around 270.

The keepers and breeders of the rarer Agapornis species have been well represented from the start and the Society has a "Rare Species Scheme" which promotes and assists the breeding of the five least common Lovebird species in UK aviculture which is open to members and non-members alike.

Society's activities, evidenced by an increase from five classes for Lovebirds (plus one shared with other general) at the National, to nine "Lovebirds only" classes in 1992. The Society introduced its own closed rings in 1991.

Lovebird Society England
Calvin Bradley
212 Jayshaw Avenue, Great Barr,
Birmingham, B43 5RH
www.lovebirdsociety.co.uk

**The African Lovebird &
Foreign Parrot Society of
Victoria, Inc.**
The Secretary, ALFPSV
Postal Address: P.O. Box 4385,
Ringwood, Victoria, 3134,
Australia
Email: alfpsv@yahoo.com

African Love Bird Society
P.O. Box 142
San Marcos
CA 92079-0142
USA

MUTAVI
Research & Advice Group
Genetics Psittacine Reference Bank
http://www.euronet.nl/users/dwjgh

**The offical MUTAVI
Agapornis Page**
The website from Dirk Van den
Abeele, the author of this book:
www.agapornis.be
email: dirk@agapornis.be

Tips for lovebirds

- Keeping and breeding birds in a responsible manner is a real art.
- A young personata is exceptionally sensitive to stress so it's better not to take on very young specimens.
- Shop around before buying and visit as many breeders in your area as you can.
- It's important to use the Latin names to avoid possible confusion.
- Check feed cups carefully. Seed, husks and debris are often mistaken for feed.
- If you're looking for a tame companion you can best choose *A. roseicollis*.
- Birds need daily care and attention.
- If you separate the young just before their first flight you will be able to tame them very quickly.

- It's better not to place other types of birds together with lovebirds.
- Lovebirds are crazy about a piece of fruit, millet spray and half ripe maize and broccoli.
- A lone lovebird may over time begin to display symptoms of psychogenic disorder.
- Don't allow young to remain for too long with their parents.
- Don't use newspapers as Cage litter.
- The bigger the cage, the better.
- Poorly considered breeding crosses will produce only valueless illegitimates and endanger the purity of the species.
- Buy only young, ringed birds.